PROTOCOL:

A Testimony for Human Connection and Social Empathy;

A Forensic Analysis Tool for Differentially Assessing Vetted, Direct, Multi-Level Marketing Models from the Commonly Utilized Buzz Term "Pyramid Scheme";

A Public Exposure of the Misconceptions and Collusion of the Bullying Dynamic

Thirteen Quaint,
Analytical Essay-Snippets Addressing the
Politics of Business Relationships –
Using the Business Dynamic as a
Lens for Examining Social Interaction

–Or–

Bubble, Bubble, Target and Toil –
A Focused Commentary
on Corporate America
as Derived from
Entrepreneurial Business Modeling
and Best-Practice Advocacy

ISBN: 978-1-312-88087-0

PROTOCOL:
A Testimony for Human Connection and Social Empathy

[applying protocol to any inter-/intra-relationship, whether personal, professional, social, cultural, or international – focusing on the business dynamic, which conforms to peer, customer, financial and economic pressures within a contained environment, as a unique filter for understanding human connectivity]

Table of Contents

1. History

**"A bad system will beat
a good person every time."**
– W. Edwards Deming

The concept of business relationships mirrors history of the CEO, as well as that of consumerism in general...

You can forget about company loyalty – employees are commonly let go days/weeks/months before retirement simply to save the funds for bonuses and the illusion of the "bottom line"

The generous, and often way out of touch, CEO Golden Parachute line-item is always in place on an ensuing contract, regardless of merit or previous performance indicators

Executive bonuses are consistently paid out in spite of poor performance, poor revenue, poor Quality, poor process management [assuming they have a clue as to the nature of the phenomenon of 'process']

On the other hand, employees receive zero notice for RIF's/office closures/layoffs

These facts are givens, and they are representative of the larger corporate culture in the United States – whether you are the Mayor of San Jose who let's an 'almost' 30-year maintenance worker go, so you don't have to cover his pension, or a private company CEO who lays off a hundred or a thousand employees in order to save the stock price

Loyalty is a one-way street: you pay for your own education, you jump through hoops to climb the corporate ladder, and at any instant your contributions to the company, your solid work history, and your achievement awards are thrown out the window in favor of someone's bottom line, so that they can get their bonus and go on that vacation to the Caribbean

If you are lucky, the Senior Executive who lets you go might pronounce your name right, and if you are really lucky, your name is spelled correctly on the 14-carat gold plated imitation Rolex they hand you just before shoving you out the door

Most aren't so lucky.

2. Infrastructure – environment of support or conflict?

"Swearing is industry language.
For as long as we're alive it's not going to change.
You've got to be boisterous to get results."
– Chef Gordon Ramsay

Hell's Kitchen allegory:

Chef Ramsay may get beet red in the face, exude expletives like a water fountain, and yell at the top of his voice – not unlike a military drill instructor at boot camp – but his intensions are unmistakably direct, honest and clear: Ramsay tears down the bad habits and builds up better behaviors – with a tone that is harsh, but respectful; he breaks a lot of eggs, but creates omelets of near-perfection.

The Corporate tone is that of quiet disrespect, ripe for tension and intolerance. A slow-cooking, hostile atmosphere of discontent, wherein the worker bee of each next lower rank must constantly walk on egg shells, demeaning themselves to a status of sub-par, low Quality 'adequacy', just above the line of getting fired, and assuredly below any measure or potential of excellence – so as not to stand out – thusly subscribing to the illusion of constancy, while maintaining job security.

Shit rolls down hill – that's the most common phrase utilized when the topic of corporate infrastructure is elucidated, examined, observed, and, if one is ready to bear the brunt of major push-back, analyzed. If you are smart, you make your assessments private (very private), you do not, EVER, post your feelings on-line in some 'supposedly personal' social forum [for the entire world to see], and under no circumstances to you allow yourself to openly criticize those senior to you, the processes in place, or the work-habits of your peers. You go to work, you do the work, you leave – and you leave your work at work, and you keep your personal life separate. Period.

If you are unfortunate enough to fall victim of the greatest ruse of the turn of the last century – that process re-engineering is a concern, that Project Management is a respectable position or capacity that advocates for change that will benefit all, and that you are that one person who has demonstrated a 'gift' or 'talent' for analyzing processes – then dust of your résumé, and prepare your interview image, because you will soon find yourself in the soup line reminiscing about the good times, and telling tales nobody wants to hear regarding how you were done wrong; how it wasn't your fault; how you were set up to fail; how it was all a big mistake.

Project Management is a long-dead and over-used, disrespected, watered-down term, which once subscribed to the notion that managing transformational change was a desire of, and fully supported by, the corporate C-levels and their respective Executive underlings. "Change or die" and "Quality, Quality, Quality" were the mantras of the day, and that day has passed.

Change just means layoff, buyout, pull the "Golden Parachute" rip cord, request political and financial bailout, sail to better shores with softer, whiter sands and translucent, clear blue, warm waters – or any combination thereof, and let the mass of worker minions fall to the whim of the larger economic wind. "Change or die" means a change of venue, and a change of the office view, for the CEO, and a slow, painful, economic death for the minions by way of terminations, food stamps, unemployment lines, foreclosures and divorces.

Change can also mean you get to see yourself replaced by someone who studied in some foreign school and is paid an eighth of your salary and provided zero benefits – but if you are lucky, you might get to travel to his/her hometown overseas, so you can personally train them; if you are very, very lucky, you might get to teach at that school, so you can put more of your domestic peers out of work by training their replacements… ah, the good life!

But change means progress – and progress is good. So, instead of complaining about the circumstances of your new-found unemployment status, you might consider starting your own company, and competing with the bastard who let you go. Let the lawyers fight over the proposed enforceability of the 'non-compete' clause you were so foolish to have signed on your first day because you were desperate to find a good job that would one day fizzle into a wet dream.

As for the notion of work itself – especially in the modern information age – you might want to get your head out of your ass, and realize that the industrial age paradigm of a solid day's work equals a solid day's pay and a solid amount of deserved respect, was a ship that sunk back in the 1970's. The efficiency (not process, but capacity) experts reported this sinking to the C-levels back in the early 1990's, and if you are a dedicated, loyal, dependable, hard-working, bright, determined, results-oriented worker, then you've been doing two day's-worth of two people each day for half the value-rate your parents were paid, and exactly zero respect – and you've been behaving in this naïve fashion right alongside your more savvy peers, who do "just enough to get by" [translation: about one-tenth of your productivity, and as for that other metric, it's about time you simply forget ever using that term "Quality" ever again in this context] and "don't raise any eyebrows" of the department heads.

With regard to metrics, let us also be clear: workers are measured by productivity levels if you are in a trade, but if you are in an office environment, you are measured by only two standards: your appearance (which is covered in that employee handbook you never read), and what time you showed up. If you show up on time, and wear what they tell you, you'll do just fine right up until the moment you get your pink slip (which will happen before you get a chance to retire – remember, your pension is not yours; it is a place-holder for tax purposes for Executive bonuses, and their vacation trips are far more important than your mortgage) – everything else is subjective and explained away in the multitude of reports and meetings and charts and easily-manipulated data. Show up, look the part (because image is EVERYTHING in our society), and keep your mouth shut.

Corporate infrastructure is in place for one purpose, and one purpose only: to perpetuate corporate culture, which means that C-levels are the superior class, and if you are reading this pamphlet, odds are high against any notion that you are one of them. If 'car payment' and 'child education fund' and 'healthcare expense' are phrases you utter – you are not one of them. Executives hand out the marching orders, and your job is to show up, pretend to do some work, and not let the door hit your ass on the way out each day; repeat Monday through Friday. Making waves and breaching policy is the stuff of fairy tales and over-budgeted Hollywood movies – you do this only if you want to know how hot the soup is that they serve to the homeless. And your MBA does not qualify you for a free cup of coffee with that soup.

3. Hiring Practices

The girlfriend complex – "not good enough for other women, not good enough for me"... wedding-ring attractant: wear one, and the ladies will fall over themselves, and each other, to buy you a drink.

The same concept, that nobody publicly admits to, is applicable and prudent in the hiring process – if you are currently employed, you are a good candidate for poaching. If you know someone in the company who can speak to your ability to show up, look the part, and keep your mouth shut, then your hire-ability has just increased exponentially. If you are unemployed, then the grim truth is both brutally blunt and overwhelmingly uncaring: your chances of getting a call after replying to that posting is slim-to-none – and every month that passes translates to a 10% reduction in those chances. At one year, you may as well go back to school and learn another trade, because, just like in the dating scene, if you were really that good at your former position, you'd still be employed... right?! And 'layoff' is just code for letting many people go (hurts your chances for suing for wrongful termination) who were just like you: they just showed up, looked the part, and were not worthy enough to retain in some vital capacity.

The HR managers don't want sufficient experience – that's a threat to their department personnel – they want the "just enough to make do experience" that can be held at arm's length with the requisite "you don't know enough yet to make that decision" script. The term "skill-set" is a list of qualities that everyone has common knowledge of, can speak to, and never actually performs. And you really need to stop using the term "Quality" already – remove it from any line-item on your résumé, and do not utter it in a phone interview.

4. Bullying

Bullying is NOT simply/merely a phenomenon about the individual! Bullying stems from cultural reinforcement, cliquing – an emotional transference of frustration culminating from a series of situations for which the individual has no training or tools to handle him-/herself... no one really gets out of the 5th grade political dynamic, and that pre-pubescent period in everyone's life is the training ground for learning such concepts as "pecking order," "abuse" (physical, verbal and emotional), and "image."

Bullying is, in fact, a facet/component of "leadership training" – often encouraged by the dynamic... teachers/parents turn a blind eye to the subtle indicator markers (assuming they are aware of them to begin with, and at that, present enough to notice their common manifestation), and only address the overt incidents as they arise – and only if their respective children are involved.

Bullying relies on intimidation – if the 'bully' actually has to use physical force, then they lose pecking order bragging status among the leadership class. Bullying is the foundation for political behavior, as it draws directly against the socio-emotional account of peer pressure.

Bullying is quite simply a 'predatory' tactic. Predatory behavior relies on establishing an image of a strong position, and attacking any position perceived as weaker, usually through verbal harassment. And if you stand up to a bully, then you risk drawing attention from your peers as "one of those who goes against the grain," which translates quickly into "you are not a team player."

The bullying dynamic is staged by society to be a "losing scenario" whether you subjugate yourself, or stand up for yourself: a Set Up To Fail, double-bind situation. Remember, the respective bully is in leadership training, and nobody - not your teachers, not your peers, and definitely not your future bosses - wants you to disrupt the status quo.

If American culture really wants to get rid of the "bullying" dynamic, it has to overtly support and defend any who "whistle-blow," "swim against the stream," "stand out," "question arbitrary decisions," or "question authority" - and that's not likely to happen, ever, considering that so much of corporate and formal politics depends on keeping just those types of people under their thumbs, or out of the light, and so much of 'status-quo' and social stratification depends on keeping people in their assigned place.

Bullying is the peer-pressure-derived tool specifically utilized to ensure social compliance. The police use it, the CEO's use it, your boss uses it, and his/her boss uses it, and so on, and so forth. This is not social engineering – it is a phenomenon present throughout history, and part of the social fabric.

Once a bully-bullee relationship is established, the bully <u>must</u> institute a measured level of consistent inter-personal terrorism: the threat of violence mixed with occasionally backing up that threat with physical interaction (often with peer assistance) – the violence itself is ever-present, and exists on an emotional-trigger level directed at the victim. Such a state of being is necessary in order to maintain the dynamic, or it will collapse – especially as the kids grow older/larger and physical reinforcement becomes more risky for the bully.

Is there an expressly identifiable solution to bullying? No, and yes.

> First, as it is becoming more and more commonplace, the concept of 'cyber-bullying' must be recognized as merely an extension of bullying with a terrifyingly modern, technological reach and potency – simply a transference of the dynamic to a newly defined forum, but no different in its essence and level of intensity – with the crux and kernel of the inherent/intrinsic dynamic held intact.

> Second, from a socially accepted, peer-oriented and adult supported (collusion by way of status quo participation), again, it must be recognized that bullying is simply an

unofficial form of expected 'pecking order actualization' [remember, bullies are often themselves bullied by other, more powerful bullies with higher status], and further, that the dynamic follows subtle, covert, intimidation cues deemed necessary as a basis for 'leadership' indoctrination. Therefore, on a socio-cultural level, the answer to the question of a cure is an unequivocally resounding "no."

However, a third, quite hopeful point: on an individual level, resides an absolute and definitive "yes," which is clearly self-evident, with the introduction of martial arts training to the children:

1. The discipline expressly levels the field of interaction by increasing confidence in the targeted victim, and simultaneously increasing the risk for the bully. Remember, bullies are predators by default, and rely primarily on the 'threat' of violence in order to sustain a tone of constant and consistent terrorism. Risk to a predator is like garlic and/or sunlight to a vampire.

2. Further, martial arts training instills a sense of presence, self-discipline, and, perhaps most importantly, the

outwardly projected value of respect from and for both victim and bully by way of self-respect cultivation.

3. Lastly, martial arts training targets the root cause of bullying behavior: that demonstrative sense of frustration – by providing him/her with a tool to handle the unfortunate environment impressed upon children: socio-political corruption, derived from and aimed at establishing an arbitrary pecking order, on behalf of which parents, teachers and bosses unwittingly collude.

Would martial arts training, if universally applied, 'cure' the social disease? Not likely, as it operates on an individual (or small group), case-by-case basis. However, each respective case erodes the foundation for the faux-leadership premise, and to great extent. Also, the more widespread its practice, the more of an underlying, pervasively perceived risk by a would-be bully, who would be forced into a sense of increased caution and need for self-preservation. Remember: bullies are predatory-cowards, with no self-respect, only pretending to be leaders.

5. Authority

Authority is the investment made by stakeholders (C-levels and/or owners) into management. It is the breeding ground for confidence in a particular manager or team, and the extension of that confidence in the form of validation.

Without express authority, a manager can forget about getting strong participation by team members or other departments – regardless of the actual or perceived benefit that could potentially result from action performed on behalf of that respective manager's directions/instructions.

Simply put, without explicitly called out authority – the backing by stakeholders, direct and public – any effort toward action-item tasking is rendered moot; a complete waste of time.

6. Perception and Credibility

Perception of a manager, and credibility allotted to the same, is presented by the team in direct proportion to the authority invested by stakeholders. Regardless of merit or past performance, the team (as well as any cross-departmental contributors) will simply dismiss any potentially positive attributes and literally sit and wait for the "green light" to move forward with any real effort.

7. Transferring Credibility / Edification

Edification is the backbone, the contract, the foundation for credibility... this is where authority meets team recognition... it is the handshake/acknowledgement of qualification: "I trust him/her, so you can."

It must be noted, however, that current policy seeks out image over substance: and to this extent, the well-qualified candidates are screened out until transference is both publically and formally displayed. It is no different from hiring practices – in fact, it may be considered as 'internal hiring' of sorts, especially when the "girlfriend complex" (previously explicated) comes into play.

How an individual is introduced to the group or department, and by whom, sets the status reference marker as well as the tone for future interaction. People simply work harder for those they believe are 'important' – or, look the part.

8. Differential Examinations:

Excellence v. Perfection

> The 'pursuit of perfection' is a fool's errand at best, and its habit is likely a root cause for OCD. Pursuit of excellence, however, is something else altogether: it suggests that we seek out improvements where-ever they may be, and utilize them when-ever discovered, especially in the areas of efficiency, process and Quality. You don't kill yourself over it, you just make sure you insert it into the existing procedural tasking, and let it systemically evolve without adding any more burden or bandwidth – more likely, it will save an incredible amount of time and effort, while increasing production exponentially, and sustaining or further reinforcing high Quality

Education v. Work Experience

> It was once the definitive corporate standard that if one were to progress up through the ranks, then he/she would attain a corresponding formal degree: Bachelors to get to Manager or Director; Masters to get to V.P. or C-Level. The contemporary standard (post-2000) is to focus on job skills and diluted certifications, and dismiss formal education as "purely academic", "irrelevant", and "unnecessary", and further, to

consider degrees as mere pieces of paper that result from an "academic hobby."

Degrees are now respected as mere trophies for those with high, faux-blue-blood status, and if a blue- or white-collar worker gets a degree, that must mean they harbor delusions of grandeur or desire greater compensation, and such notions must be extinguished as recognizable achievements for the working class. "Formal education" is deemed non-applicable to the work environment, wherein there exists only respect for hard work, which leads to many years of "real" experience – besides, you might make your peers feel uncomfortable, and in turn, they might accuse you of "thinking you're the smartest person in the room." If you wish to sustain a peaceful working environment, you might reconsider openly disclosing your formal, "academic" pieces of paper.

Any discussion regarding the practice of formal education is especially important to me. Of course, having invested in both a Bachelors and a Masters degree, I could be considered more than biased – and that is prudent. However, I also have had extensive military training (nearly two of my six years in service was devoted to training schools and On the Job Training), as well as OJT in every single corporate environment to which I have been exposed.

With regard to experience itself, I have come to recognize that without lessons learned, experience is merely routine.

With regard to formal education, I find that without applied experience, such "book knowledge" is rendered to a status of trivia, and reduced to the level of academia-centric. I believe that formal education can be exceptional if it is framed within an applied structure, such as Engineering, or at the very least, the underlying theoretical components are explicated 'with respect' to application – such as noting that the act of deriving a theorem or principle may be academic on the surface, but exposes the practitioner to the appreciation of pattern recognition and cross-functional application (behaviors which must be used to be gained, just like lifting weights to gain muscle mass).

One common side-discussion involves "inherent talent" as opposed to "study," and I strongly believe the analogy to be both prudent, apt, and adept in its presentation with regard to "formal education v. work experience": some say they can pick up a guitar, or sit at a piano, and "play music" after listening to a rendition just once, or, learn to play difficult pieces within a very short period – and therefore, formal study/education is not necessary.

I would counter from a personal experience: I observed, first-hand, one of my musical mentors, who applauded a student's brilliant performance of Beethoven's "Für Elise," which was accurate, precise and conformed to strict, classical standard, yet still "original and emotive" – then promptly sat down, and began to play the same herself in front of the class, and asked the audience to call out rhythms, which we did... bossa nova, rock and roll, gypsy, salsa, jazz... and on the fly (or rather, 'off the cuff', extemporaneously), our mentor would switch up this famous classical piece, providing for an exotic rendition the likes of which may never be exposed outside of a formal classroom (or private, formal study) context.

Now, to do so, she had to change not only the rhythm, as requested, but also the chord progressions in order to match the quality of the rhythms they conform to, within a double-context of both the transition and the overall classical piece itself – all without missing a beat. "That is what applied theory gives you – the ability to successfully adapt in real time to changing conditions within a defined framework." And you can't apply theory, if you don't formally learn theory to begin with.

It should also be stated that most OJT, even though it takes place in the work place, is grounded in best practices, work experience within context, and lessons learned, all of which makes it (OJT) applied theory, even if not formally taught in a classroom environment.

I would assert that to be a truly strong business person, to adapt successfully to changing business environments, and subsequently profit from the same, one should espouse the appreciation of, attainment of, and respect for the critical, 3-legged stool of Personal/Professional Development, being:

- Formal Education
- Cross-Functional Pattern Recognition
- Best Practices / OJT

Generalist v. Technologist/Specialist

"Modern science is characterized by its ever-increasing specialization, necessitated by the enormous amount of data, the complexity of techniques and of theoretical structures within every field. Thus science is split into innumerable disciplines continually generating new sub-disciplines. In consequence, the physicist, the biologist, the psychologist and the social scientist are, so to speak, encapsulated in their private universes, and it is difficult to get word from one cocoon to the other..."
– Ludwig von Bertalanffy

Given that I am a STRONG advocate for, and believer in, General Systems Theory, and given that my primary business field is the systemically-oriented discipline of Project Management (the non-diluted, accurately applied and non-corrupted form, which you may glean from my treatise on advanced Project Management: "S.U.I.T.E. PCISTM"), I am highly sensitive to any manner of erosion to process capture, analysis, digestion, re-engineering and re-integration. Therefore, I am equally offended by, and immunized against, the current trend of forcing specializing attitudes onto any who seek to learn more about the business dynamic.

The technologist (technician, specialist) falls victim to the commonly held notion and commonly subscribed-to misnomer that a given set of sub-patterns are unique to a respective dynamic – an unsupported, uninformed, highly insufficient, and highly contagious supposition that violates all levels of philosophical foundation, the laws of physics, as well as sociological/psychological, pure logic, and mathematical principles.

The generalist subscribes to cross-functional pattern recognition and integration: learns to break down process components, parse and re-configure, build components back into larger processes, and repeat. The sensitivity is general in vision, but highly focused and methodical in application: macro assimilate; building-block digest; micro re-engineer.

This concept of general systems infusion is relevant not only to personal effort, but also to the pedagogy inherent:

- Learn how to re-engineer

- Apply reciprocally to learning process
  - Learn how to learn more efficiently
    - Apply learning how to learn to learning how to learn – fold process back onto itself – exponential efficiency potentials
    - Faster and wider assimilation, greater recognition and association capability, easier identification of cross-functional patterns
- Apply to multiple arenas
  - Develop personal gravitation to polymathic attributes
- Devise systemic polymathic engine

"We are seeking another basic outlook: the world as an organization. This would profoundly change the categories of our thinking and influence our practical attitudes. We must envision the biosphere as a whole with mutually reinforcing or mutually destructive interdependencies."
– Ludwig Von Bertalanffy

Pyramid Scheme v. Solid Marketing Principles

[or, "Standard" v. Direct Marketing practices analyzed, explicated, and explained]…

A true "pyramid" scheme is based on the Ponzi scheme, but with multiple legs of recruiting –> all monies are based solely on the practice of recruitment, with no incentive or commission attached explicitly to a product or service. A 'scheme' is a ploy; a tactic.

Schemes have an appropriately egregious connotation: "taking advantage of someone." Schemes also comprise an equally prudent and devious denotation: "duping or conning someone." Schemes are to filtered out by way of recognition (litmus testing) and subsequently avoided at all costs – common sense dictates this expressly and explicitly. But do note, that Direct Marketing, so long as the commissions and emphasis is on the product/service, on not on the act of recruiting, is not to be categorized as a 'scheme.'

Madoff is among the most recent of these vicious Predators who practiced "Pyramid-style" Ponzi scheme, disguised as a stock investment model –> not once did his model ever pass muster or litmus to the trained forensic analyst, and his activities were reported early and often to the S.E.C., among other government agencies, but to no avail, as Madoff's "image" and "status" was respected more than the evidence. The market caused Madoff's eventual demise, leaving the authorities scrambling to find justifiable reasons for not acting sooner (when the evidence of his criminal actions was delivered to them on a silver platter).

Most lay people, and even many who proclaim business savvy, lack the understanding of the true nature of "pyramid" schemes, and balk at the very mention of it. These very same will quickly label multi-level-marketing models – which are highly successful, often perform in outstanding fashion in the stock market, and are based on solid product and service offerings – as "pyramid" simply because they don't want to be viewed as ignorant, even though they have no capacity for due diligence with regard to the appropriate, minimal level of basic analysis required to offer a valid and validated, evidence-based assessment, and as such, they quickly use an emotive-provoking (fallacy) buzz word which they hope will deflect the audience from further pursuit of the subject matter, allowing them to save face and embarrassment.

The disdain toward direct marketing is similar to the stigma spread about regarding on-line, for-profit schools – which are considered merely, and incorrectly, a modern version of correspondence curricula. Even though in many cases such on-line study is better representative of communication with globally distributed workforces, and is often more rigorous, more advanced, more relevant to current situations, and more applicable, and often achieved through practical, live case-study, it is deemed 'inferior' to traditional, brick-and-mortar programs – an assessment derived solely on the basis of buzzword propaganda, and further reinforced by way of culturally elitist association.

The use of the term "pyramid" alone, outside of product/service context, is misleading at best, if not outrageously misrepresentative -> for all companies utilize a pyramid of authority, status, and compensation

My advice is two fold:

1) Take a class on business models, take a class on contract law, take a class on the history of consumerism, and take a class on business ethics – learn, from real mentors, about real scrutiny that is fact-based on not merely opinion; and establish a set of litmus tests to immunize yourself such that you do not fall victim to such tactics or ploys.

2) Further educate yourself, by way of personal development, in order to become more socially aware – differentiate between duplicitous, hurtful schemes from the well-established practice of Network Marketing: an advantageous, validated, vetted, scrutinized ethically, legally and procedurally (by agency and law), health- and wealth-building paradigm/business model.

Modern Networking models are simultaneously both direct and multi-level in nature:

Direct – in the sense that the individual associate is an independent business owner-representative, operating directly between the producer and the consumer, with no other middlemen involved

Multi-Level – commissions are paid out in advance, and split between the individual associate and his/her 'up-line' (recruiting tree)

Take heed: Network and Direct Marketing business models are rising up in viable fashion at an exponential rate within the modern, on-line, social-networking age. They are prudent, profitable, comprising systems which are easy to duplicate, have been around since the dawn of business practice and word-of-mouth credibility, and are here to stay.

The following represent multi-level marketing models, which might, to the untrained eye, and absent any prudent investigation, "seem" like a scheme, but are actually definitively legal and appropriate business practices:

Google, Yahoo espouse network marketing –

payments from 3rd-parties based on respective sites traffic / reaches / touches / engagements / click-thru's

Amazon employs network marketing –

3rd-parties store material and pay for delivery direct to customer (much like the parent MLM company), and the 3rd-parties pay Amazon a commission for presence in the on-line market, for credibility (ratings – word of mouth), and validation

YouTube espouses network marketing –

the more followers/memberships/traffic on an account's page, the more commission paid to that account

real estate brokers harbor a true network marketing dynamic

hire commission-based agents

who hire commission-based financial reps

independent musicians are the archetype example of network marketing

hand out flyers

promote shows to other musicians – request "word of mouth" follow-up on their behalf, with mutual assurance to reciprocate

trade skill sets in open market (session work for kick-back on production fees; referral incentives) any dynamic that promotes commission-based delivery or drives "word of mouth" espouses credibility derived from network marketing –

"word of mouth" IS network marketing, by definition:

every time you recommend a movie, a mechanic, a novel, a new restaurant, a dentist, etc., etc., to a friend, you are an unpaid network marketer

and every corporate advertisement on T.V., whether a trailer for an upcoming movie, or a slot for a "dining out" experience, or a spot showing kids enjoying themselves at a theme park, has the express expectation and sole purpose to generate "word of mouth" – thusly tapping into the interactive device known as the "mother's recipe"; the "credibility by association" dynamic

Television and radio advertising which utilizes a referral phrase ("tell them that Joel at radio KXYZ sent you!"), or that attach a discount to a promotion code ("the code word is 'guitar'"; "the number of the day is 4321"), from which commissions and/or referral fees are paid, are employing network marketing techniques, allowing the marketer to take credit for the sale and receive the payment due – payment which is only dispersed upon sale (one of the defining attributes of Direct Marketing, and why this business model is so successful)

The practices of the likes of Facebook, Google, Amazon, and YouTube have firmly established – and subsequently leveraged by "standard" brick and mortar companies – Direct, Multi-Level Network Marketing is a tried-and-true, proven concept, based on genuine human interaction, and it is the wave of the future

Outside sales, even if salaried, is actually a network marketing capacity, with a primary role to sensitize prospects to a new technology, a new product (even if merely "new packaging"), a new service, a new bundle (supposedly to save cost for the customer, but actually only saves the company logistical and marketing costs), or, of course, the all-too-common "hurry up and buy now before it's too late" scripted rhetoric

the "cult approach" to behavior

behavioral conditioning using directed marketing principles

I used to subscribe to the notion that the terms "cult" and "brainwashing" were most appropriately applied to:

- those fringe, quasi-religious groups who ran off into the desert or jungle and brainwashed their followers (likely due to television news broadcasts of the likes of the Reverend Jim Jones and his respective followers, and similar incidents, from when I was a young, impressionable child); or, to

- victims of "black box" CIA operations.

However, the same could be attributed to the indoctrination of formal college study (refer back to Education v. Indoctrination above), military boot camp environments [which I personally believe to be a very positive experience of breaking down bad habits and instilling discipline – IFF attained and reinforced through sincere, positive framework, and IFF the individual actually comes out the back end as "built back up"; not merely torn down, as can be the case], and indeed, the corporate culture and environment that is pushed onto those of us who must seek a living "by wages":

every manufacturer that conducts a safety meeting/circle at the beginning of each shift; every retailer (Best Buy, Wal-Mart) that conducts a sales pitch meeting / "huddle" / "inspiring get-together" just prior to opening the store

often focusing on a particular commission-based / quota-based product, e.g.

- "supplementary insurance" (such as pushed onto consumers of popular electronics)

- "extended warranty" on used car sales, or other such products

"If you know anyone..." network marketing

Commission percentage incentive rewards

Paid out at point of sale or recruitment

Split between the "finder", the "recruiter", the "recruiting manager" and the "recruiting company" by definition, this is absolutely and definitively multi-level marketing

"...who needs a good used car – have them call me, and I'll cut you in."

"...who needs a good lawyer – have them call me, and I'll cut you in."

"...who is looking to buy/sell a house – have them call me, and you'll get a finder's fee."

"...who can fill the rec (a 'requisition' – skill or capacity requirement, often targeting high tech, senior executive, or CEO capacities/skill-sets, or, highly specific certifications, such as nurses) – have them call me, and I'll pay you a finder's fee."

Another common thread, often heard in forums, resonates far and wide with regard to reaching out to prospective recruits: what if they believe they can't do what you do? – to which the following advice is both sound and prudent:

"First, step out of your comfort zone – you may surprise yourself with what you CAN really do. Second, perhaps you aren't 'the best' at recruiting or selling product – the goal is to find someone who has this talent, and recruit them to network on your behalf. And third, remember that successful systems involve activities that are inherently duplicate-able."

Here are some special notes regarding the business of Direct, Multi-Level Network Marketing:

1) Apply sincere scrutiny – remember to do your research and vet each new opportunity against a set of prudent litmus qualifications:

  a. Research the company – its reputation, and that of its Executives

  b. Research the product/service – does it meet a clearly defined need in the marketplace?

c. Is the price-point for the product or service appropriately set for the target client base?

d. Is the web-site messaging clearly established?

2) Consider these respective mantras as informed context:

a. Retail and Real Estate Mantra

"Location, Location, Location"

b. Marketing Mantra ("the 4 P's")

- Product (or Service).
- Place.
- Price.
- Promotion.

c. Project Management Mantra

"Quality, Quality, Quality"

d. Entrepreneurship/Network Marketing Mantra

"Personal Development, Personal Development, Personal Development"

Lastly, I would like to personally assert here a particular observation which might be considered enlightening:

Directed Marketing [a.k.a. Direct Sales, or Multi-Level Marketing (within the context of commission compensation)], which is a <u>focused endeavor between two discrete parties</u>, meaning, one individual passing specific knowledge and information to another person directly and efficiently – can be distinctly, and expressly differentiated from its counter mass-marketing practice of

Blanket (Television / Radio / Web page) *Onslaught Advertising*, which is indirect in application, loosely informative, rife with caveats ("some studies have shown…", "may produce side-effects such as…", "may cause…", etc.), and leads members of its audience to a phone number, web site, or brick-and-mortar retail locale, where they met by a phone tree, a click tree, or an equally uninformative sales person – who might be just eager enough to point the customer to an aisle then leave that prospect in a state of anxiety and frustration, so he/she can go on that "all-important" smoke-break, <u>unless</u>, of course, if that sales person makes a commission on the sale and/or is under the constraint of meeting a particular deadline or quota, in which case he/she is overly eager to overwhelm the consumer with high pressure, NLP sales tactics, gain confidence, and upsell to a more costly version of the product that the consumer didn't need in the first place. It is this particular drill of "target the victim-consumer" that is often attributed to Direct Marketing, while it is whole-heartedly practiced by "standard" blitz-advertising / sales floor, script-oriented schemes which are run by middle-men, whose primary stake is invested in tapping into an existing revenue stream, covering operational overhead and introducing unnecessary risk/cost to the dynamic, and whose primary agenda is to separate the consumer from his/her wallet.

Personally, I have grown to trust the more efficient, and more honest, *Direct Marketing* model, which informs the end consumer, and delivers the product or service directly, without any middle-man. Having spent the better part of two decades as a sales person on the retail floor (electronics, clothing, shoes, and multiple home improvement departments), having run the background marketing, supply chain, logistics, operations, customer service and accounting processes for retail, and, having researched, practiced, analyzed, evaluated and critiqued Direct Marketing for a short time, I think my experience is sufficient to make such observational claims, and support them with evidence and argument. Direct Marketing is by no means a perfect system, but as many, such as Jim Rohn, among others, have often stated, it is a better system than "the more-accepted standard."

"Profit in business comes from repeat customers, customers that boast about your project or service, and that bring friends with them."
– W. Edwards Deming

Recommended Viewing:

"Rise of the Entrepreneur" DVD, Eric Worre
http://www.riseoftheentrepreneur.org/

"Perfect Storm" DVD, Darnell Self

Recommended Listening:

"Building Your Network Marketing Business" CD, Jim Rohn

Recommended Reading:

"Think and Grow Rich", Napoleon Hill
http://en.wikipedia.org/wiki/Think_and_Grow_Rich

9. Behavioral Conditioning

Programming behavior –

Everyone knows about the frog in hot water, yet we still have ATM/hidden fees – or worse, open fees that have become "ok, and customary by default, usage and commonplace precedent."

But what is even more egregious is the fact that many of the monthly account fees (for electronic banking statements) are, at best, misrepresentative, and should be questioned with regard to their inherent legality. Such electronic status reports actually piggy back (at no cost to the institution) an existing, necessary set of communication channels.

These fees are pure revenue, meaning that they have no associated risk or operational cost associated, and stem from a not-so-subtle practice of conversion (legally defined: theft), which is based on ignorance of a modern, technological capability, and comprise two discrete objectives:

1. Apply pressure for direct deposit and/or increased ATM usage – both of which are relationship/dynamic-restrictive, behavioral reinforcers; and

2. Generate revenue tapping feeds (base-lining) for executive bonuses

10. Identities, Personalities, and Reputations

**"Research shows that the climate
of an organization influences
an individual's contribution
far more than the
individual himself."**
– W. Edwards Deming

Masks of the Business Arena [personnel usually wear three or more]...

'negatives' are fully supported, culturally, by the business infrastructure, and lead to quick promotion and/or retention...

'positives' are risky, in the sense that they: a) are unsettling to those who use the 'negatives'; b) take a very long time to realize promotion, unless Image is validated; and c) can actually lead to vulnerable status; dismissal...

one can shift from positive to negative, and vice-versa, simply by espousing personal development in concert with the underlying values inherent: positive – integrity, trust, honor, temerity, diligence, discipline, self-respect, loyalty, perseverance; negative – betrayal, deception, distrust, disrespect, copout, insecurity...

however, once you head down a particular path, there is an exponential reinforcement for continuing down that selected, particular direction, derived from cultural and personal incentives, and any attempts at changing direction becomes correspondingly difficult...

respect for others stems from self-respect...

competence stems from recognition of technical aspects married to skilled facets, meaning, if you don't know the method, learn it and/or hire someone who has a solid handle on it – do not fear competence, fear the result of not attaining it, instead of finding a cover-up...

negativity bleeds over into diminished productivity levels, reduced product Quality – and it is just as important to note that it is reflected clearly in private, personal relationships/dynamics; their children become bullies and cyberbullies...

one might believe the topic to be entirely 'gray-area', however, there are two aspects to strongly consider: 1) personalities comprise skill sets – and they are 'developed', in the sense that one can become more or less joyful by its daily practice or neglect; and 2) these identity traits feed on each others' energy and gravitate toward commonality/similarity...

This is probably the best juncture to take a moment for reflection. As one seeks to discover, then establish, then ground, then assert his or her identity, it may very well be of value to determine what would be considered a truly 'successful' accomplishment within the framework of 'identity' itself. To that end, I can only look to my own perspective, as I look through the various personalities with whom I have interacted over the years, filtering out those of whom I seek to emulate, espouse, or avoid – and with equal measure, I believe that my own values, the set of which I use as a litmus house that filtering mechanism, can best be summed with the following two quotes when "success" is the determining factor:

"To laugh often and love much; to win the respect of intelligent persons and the affection of children; to earn the approbation of honest citizens and endure the betrayal of false friends; to appreciate beauty; to find the best in others; to give of one's self; to leave the world a bit better..."
– most likely the work of one
Bessie Anderson Stanley, circa 1904
[though often mis-attributed to Ralph Waldo Emerson,
and somewhat less often to Robert Louis Stevenson –
http://emerson-legacy.tamu.edu/Ephemera/Success.html]

"Do the work that's nearest,
Though it's hard at times,
Helping when we meet them,
Lame dogs over styles."
-anonymous
[as reiterated to me, daily, by my
late Great Grandfather Osborne,
as I sat on his knee, listening to his
stories of World War I, and teaching
me Morse Code]

I leave it up to each of you to decide what your respective mix is, as well as that of your peers, friends, vendors, managers, and executives

increased empathy + <- - -> - reduced capacity for human connectivity

The Poker Player

Never gives up his/her hand, hides any social tells, often hard to read, often observant, does not like threatening tones to be directed at him/her

The Charlatan

Manages to Image; constructs gray-area narratives and hides in the ambiguity

The Con-Artist

Falsifies friendships to gain an angle; primary agenda is to climb the ladder at all costs – even betraying peers; beguiles; utilizes mirroring and other associated NLP tactics

The Busy Bee / The "8-Hour" Task-Spreader

Utilizes deflection to dissuade investigation into his/her lack of performance; the "impossible" and "no time" conceptualist

The Enabler

Overlooks lack in performance Quality of subordinates (and sometimes even the same in superiors, in deference)

The Entrepreneur

Seeks out solutions targeting "impossible" problems and efficiency dynamics to develop profitable, secret sauce concepts for start-ups – a true entrepreneur not only finds a new product / service / adaptation, but also a new method or means for development or production or distribution, which serves as the basis for the 'secret sauce' – providing for increased profitability within the underlying processes as well as within the overtly presented form-factor

The Hyper-Criticizer

utilizes 'ad hominem' attacks at will; often disguises subtle bullying intent/tone/agenda to be faux-supportive: "I'm just trying to help"

The Advocate

Takes on burden (sometimes with little or no notice); works late, on weekends; meets issues head-on; takes responsibility for not achieving desired goals; takes brunt of criticism on behalf of team; bears weight and absorbs bandwidth (and heavy lifting) on behalf of internal/external customers, clients and co-workers; seeks out advice from Subject Matter Experts and Analysts to arrive at solutions to dire situations; is quite often an overworked, underappreciated, and unrecognized 'Empowerer'

The Backseat Driver

Attacks peers incessantly with fallacy-ridden comments; often confused with an 'Empowerer' – but the key illuminator is that the latter speaks strictly to process improvement, not to the owner of the activity; uses subtle, disparaging, and sometimes intimidating tone

The Empowerer

Finds tools to aid others; "how can I help you?" along with "sure, I can come in over the weekend (or stay late in the office) to ensure that the project gets finished on time" are commonly heard phrases; subscribes to continuous process improvement; manages to Quality; lends cross-departmental assistance; seeks out more efficient means to accomplish goals and increase productivity; will either find a solution (problem-solving development) directly, find a third-party who can derive a solution, or help you to find your own solution – or any combination thereof

The Heel Chaser

Rides on the backs of others' innovations, solutions, conceptualizations, and efforts – latching onto fragments of conversation in order to piece together a pseudo-narrative suggestive of original thought, and thereby mold a faux-vision that is supposedly worthy of merit – while in reality, they provide a zero-sum value. The Heel Chaser is a derivative, sub-component skill set to the Back Seat Driver

The Analyst

Utilizes a host of algorithmic utilities to establish trends: litmus / scrutiny; pattern recognition; parsing / parallel work assignment

The Blind Believer

Never questions protocol, policy or procedure – hides behind that position, as well as rules and regulations, in faux-support of management

The Predator

"your day has finally come -
so wear the hat and do the dance
and let the suit keep wearing you...
this year you'll sit and take it
and you will like it -
it's the gentle art of making enemies"
– Faith No More, Rock Group

Preys on the following victim categories

Older generations

Reverse mortgage schemes

Religious donations – assurance for salvation from sin; a place in heaven

Systemic (by design and manipulation)

Finance arena

Rules/Legal changes -> Shorting Scheme -> Bubble -> prescribed wealth-building model to benefit wealthy; destroy savings for lower class individuals and pension plans

Bailout solutions politically attained by way of pressure and intimidation

Indemnity from criminal charges

Executive bonuses as a reward for orchestrated failure

Low Income

Real Estate -> Interest Rate Balloon Scheme -> Bubble -> prescribed wealth-building model to benefit wealthy; foreclosures for lower class individuals and families

Dupe-able Uninformed Investors

Hedge Funds -> shorting mechanism

Ponzi Scheme – the "Madoff" model

The Orchestrator

Makes up for incompetence and insecurity; utilizes a host of techniques to manipulate entire groups: sabotage; sewing the seeds of resentment and rejection; duplicity; throwing others under bus; emasculation; betrayal; pathological deceit; coercion; collusion; gaslighting; targeting reputations; berating, subtly demeaning tones; humiliation; double-bind routines;

Instills toxicity into the environment; corrupts relationships; utilizes rumor-based hysteria generation and molding; separates/isolates; employs the "Cinderella" tool – bogging subordinates down with minutia and trivial tasking; retains an off-putting position of "inability to please": changing parameters and intentional SUTFS; outright, often overt (though not called out) intimidation/bullying

The Modern CEO

Their respective Business Savvy should be scrutinized and measured against Technical Brilliance, but rarely is

Promote an environment conducive to complacency

Covet mediocrity, favoring consistency to excellence – wasting valuable dollars laying off expertise and mastery and professionalism in the name of pennies to the bottom line

Their route to leadership is often predetermined, elitist, nepotistic, and rarely subscribes to merit or capability... historical trends dilemma, image[2]: espousing the image of image... Technical backgrounds; then Financial; then Marketing;

then, a route which fully departs mode of inspiration in favor of manipulation – a disposition which worked in favor of industrial-age models, but is failing exponentially in the modern, fast-changing, cyberspace-impacted social-networking age

Culturally reinforced and expected level of approved narcissism / display of superiority complex / psychopathy / dissociation / disconnected attitudes and behaviors

11. Argumentative Foundations

Predictive Analytics

Finding the holes, peaks, valleys, trends, anomalies

What can be, What can't be, What must be

Fitting the evidence to the theory – or resetting parameters to a more appropriate context within which to capture the evidence

Pudding of Proof – looking to where the numbers take us, the evidence, the merit… each of these calls into question the 'image' factor, speak directly to substance and Quality, and dispel any notion of cutting corners… this is the true bottom line, and is neither arbitrary nor wasteful in its pursuit

Thorough Analysis Documentation – such diligent efforts allow for solid understanding of valid metrics within the context of the process being analyzed; set the tone and foundation for positive, transformational adaptation to an ever-changing market environment [note: be equally careful to avoid "analysis paralysis" – get work done!]

12. Where does this take us as a society?

   …as a Western culture?; as 'Corporate America'?

   The future is grim, if the advanced preparation, burden absorption for the duration, and the cleanup of the aftermath of recent catastrophes [Hurricanes Katrina and Sandy, Haiti Earthquake] is any true indication of our capability to effect a purposeful response: a grand Social Intelligence failure – stemming from the reliance of inferior programs, themselves based on inadequate procedures and policies – resulting from the diminished Contributory Individual Intelligence Capacity component-quotient; from combination of the contract with mediocrity mixed with the commitment to faulty routines, which reduces neurological firings and connections, curing to a lowered individual intelligence.

   I am not talking simply about the educational system which has systemically automatonized each oncoming generation, nor merely of the physical infrastructure (e.g. bridges) that is degrading at a rate far more quickly than our 'modern' cell-phone-constrained and social media-addicted brains can arrive at a solution, but of the combinatory integration of a multitude of complacency-ridden factors that have led us down a path toward self-destruction.

We don't need any more wars on drugs or wars on terror or wars on this or that 'ism' – we need a war on mediocrity and stupidity; we need to change course, and establish a foundation for a rise to excellence. We need to learn how to foster growth; to promote a value for substance; to generate a sincere appreciation for Quality; to stop standing on each others' necks, and begin lifting others onto our shoulders.

13. So what are the corrective measures?

"It takes a revolution to make a solution."
-Bob Marley

You can't rely on government stepping in – the government is, by definition, a social engine. It is the individual, then the individual's personal circle, then the individual's larger community, and then the individual's grander network that must transform before it's too late.

The A.I.'s (Action Items) for the conscious empath in pursuit of human connectivity and a reversal of the downward spiral:

Embrace continuous process improvement

Seek out better tools for any and all activities

Pressure application vendors for better solutions

better tools and better reporting streams: greater efficiency, calculation/pivoting capability, relevance-to-extraneous ratio, auto-forwarding of digested information.

Reference best-practices

reciprocate into the dynamic by contributing your own improved segment concepts to the best-practice library for any given pattern, trade, theory – you don't have to reinvent the whole wheel, just concentrate on a spoke or the composition of the tire, or the welding, etc.

Sensitize yourself

break up routine, while immunizing yourself against any notions of mediocrity.

Marry yourself to personal development

BE PASSIONATE! Strive for professional and inter-personal excellence and mastery: wide net for goals with narrow focus for execution (as many have said, "good is the antithesis of great" – so learn to remove the "sufficient" or "good"), teach others, teach others how to teach others, recognize patterns, push into other arenas, embrace being uncomfortable, do NOT settle, challenge yourself – then increase the level/complexity of challenge.

"Work harder on yourself
than you do on your job."
– Jim Rohn

Drive Communication

introduce greater energy and effort into improving and focusing communication channel protocols/automation.

Establish an environment of respect

> exude passion, compassion, diligence, discipline and devotion.

> conform to the concept that in order to advance, one must successfully train his/her replacement – and further, that said success is not achieved until the trainee's trainee has passed evaluation.

Confirm connectivity and compassion

> recognize and support solid, empathetic values when demonstrated by others.

"The result of long-term relationships is
better and better Quality, and
lower and lower costs."
– *W. Edwards Deming*

Actionable Means toward Exponential/Influential Power

"Discipline Will Set You Free"
[breakdown of why this is so]

Discipline as a Process of Incorporation/Integration	Capability	Ability / Means	The "ize" have it:		Follow-thru as a Process of Re-Integration and Continuous Improvement
	Capability	Ability	**Conceptualize**		
				tap into creativity	
				idea generation	
				problem solutioning	
			Improvise		
				research education / training / experience	
				discover methods / best practices / precedents	
				seek out "key-opener" tools for secret sauce in other arenas	
				("spoon for vacuum sealed jar")	
				improve calculatin and test methods	
				incorporate into being	
			Devise		
				map out tasking	
				leave routine – consciously act, challenge yourself	
				plan of attack	
			Scrutinize		
				explicate hooks & triggers / patterns	
				mold and manipulate patterns into actionable models	
		Means	**Synthesize**		
				calculate / test / run logic routine / hone models	
			Synergize		
				integrate models into tool box	
			Systemitize		
				Develop matrix of accessible models	

Ability is merely a singular skill set
Capability places multiple skills sets into action to achieve predictive results

A "Problem" is merely a gap/differential between where you are, and where you want to be
  Problems should be aligned in difficulty with goal timeline
    Bite-size, immediate, actionable
    Digestible, medium-term, personal growth
    Lofty, long-term, "Supreme Goal"-oriented

Supreme Goals:
  Recycle results back into model matrix
  Further increase
    Discipline
      Capability
        Ability
        Means
  Get personal agenda just in front of the "wave of success"
    Let wave work for you:
      Systemic resonance – align with greater resources and agenda
      Wave Attractants Resonance – sweet spots and secret sauces
FILTER
  Focused Intention
  Lead Targeting [influential and predictive]
  Explicit Results

Discipline *allows the individual to adapt to any situation, under any circumstances, at any given moment*
    allows for incorporating/integrating task into current sequence without
        losing quality or interrupting schedule
    increases Ability (bandwidth/capacity; training/methodology) to **take on additional burden** with less notice
        –> on the fly, ability to go from the "impossible/massively difficult" to "extremely easy/scalable"
    increases Means to act on given task and provide meaningful, tangible results – while
        achieving all goals set by personal agenda
    and simultaneously, increases the Capability to manifest an incremental, transformational change
Translation: **Freedom**

Power is the ability to act, Exponential/Influential Power is derived from Disciplined Capability
    Credit is modern leverage
    Money is a modern contract – an incremental, fluxuating derivation of power

Rules, parameters and constraints are excellent guiedlines in any given arena – use them to your advantage!

About the Essayist:

M. Scott Campbell, MPM
is an Entrepreneur and Applied Business Theorist
http://about.me/mscottcampbell

Masters in Project Management from
Keller Graduate School of Management,
with emphases in
Change Advocacy and Process Re-Engineering

Bachelors in Arts in Rhetoric from Willamette University
with emphases in
Mathematics, Philosophy, Music

Over Two Decades of Wide, Deep and Varied Experience in:

High Tech Project Management (Software/Network)

Music (Songwriting/Performance/Production)

Marketing

Property Management

Construction

International Trade

Transportation Logistics

Equipment Management

Retail (Electronics / Home Improvement)

Military Intelligence
(Imagery Analysis; Russian Cryptologic Linguist)

Other Works from this Author:

http://www.lulu.com/spotlight/mscottcampbell

"S.U.I.T.E. PCISTM":
(Process-Centric Integrated System for Transformational Methodologies) –
A Treatise for the Advancement of the Project Management Discipline.

"Walk With Me Awhile":
Confessions of a Modern Polymath
(an intimate collection of essays, poems, criticisms, and lyrics)

"Campbell's Rhetorical Method for Writing a Novel"
(small pamphlet comprising step-by-step instructions)

TETHER Trilogy:
https://www.facebook.com/tether.trilogy

TETHER
is a quasi-non-fictional
dissertation on Cognition Theory
presented along the
superpositioned states of a(n)
treatise on Narrative / exercise in Rhetoric / thesis on Metaphor /
explication of Astrophysics / lemma on Chaos Theory /
discussion in Metaphysics / treatment of Music /
exploration of Number Theory /
arguments for
Mathematics, Philosophy and Theoretical Physics;
disguised as
an epic work,
embedded Within the fictional genres of
cyberpunk / high-fantasy / cerebral sci-fi / military-action /
mystery / urban-fantasy / horror /
human transcendentalism

Book I – "DIATRÆCVS"

Book II – "THE PŒTRÆTIVS"

Book III – "RHÆDTHIVS"

www.ingramcontent.com/pod-product-compliance
Lightning Source LLC
Chambersburg PA
CBHW021905170526
45157CB00005B/1972